MILES PRESS

Indiana University South Bend Department of English

LOVE SICK CENTURY

42 Miles Press
Editor, David Dodd Lee
ISBN 978-1-7328511-6-0 (pbk. alk. paper)

http://42miles.wordpress.com

Art Direction: Nick Kuder, Design: Sydni Gothard, Production: Paul Sizer
Cover photography courtesy of Freepik
The Design Center, Frostic School Of Art, Western Michigan University.
Printing: Sheridan Printing.

LOVE
SICK
CENTURY

POEMS
BY
ELLY
BOOKMAN

CONTENTS

Acknowledgments

Foreword by Ashley Capps

The sinister shadow of the late capitalist war machine falls on everything in Elly Bookman's debut collection, *Love Sick Century*. In the unforgettable early poem, "Privilege," the speaker sunbathes at a public pool beneath a sky filled with the "small whitenesses" of fighter jets rehearsing combat, and wryly notes: "I lie back in my chair [...] and try to become browner." The irony is as casual as it is scalding, and from this atmosphere of discomfiting malaise the poem accelerates into something more bleak:

In this sky, planes fly
low and heavy, back and
forth from the base,
practicing war. I'm afraid
I'm finally all right
knowing good things
in me have died.

Is this cynicism? Perhaps. These are poems of air strikes and warships, active shooter drills and students' "shadowy backpacks" (the poet is a teacher). Even in a poem titled "Threatless," when a male lover's hand cradles the back of the speaker's neck, something ominous menaces. But if the tone is one of cynicism, it's not the snide indifference or stony skepticism of the coarsened realist. Rather, it's the sort born of profound tenderness, and one that breeds tenderness in turn through its unfailing eye for beauty, mercy, and wonder—in spite of what it's learned about the world.

In the poem "Vivarium," with all the earnestness of John Cusack's boombox serenade in *Say Anything*, the speaker plays a thunderstorm soundtrack to a pair of pet frogs, hoping to spur them to mate. In the poem "Clamor," amidst the bombardment of television war news, the speaker recalls a single perfect soap bubble hovering behind the back of a former lover as he washes the dishes.

And in "Nocturne," the same hypervigilance that scrutinizes the lights on the home security system panel remembers too "that somewhere, someone's job / is to place tiny bulbs inside / plastic bodies, that / someone else's is to decide / that firefly color." Indeed, inside the desolate ennui of these pages, fireflies nonetheless still shimmer their plaintive SOS: "here am I. / Here am I." The best of these poems deftly captures a seething disquiet with a mastery I've not encountered since Arda Collins' virtuosic debut, *It Is Daylight*. *Love Sick Century* is both distress signal and emergency response; rest assured, help is on the way, if only these poems can find you.

1.

Today

a war started. But
thousands more were already
in bloom so it felt like
going for groceries, like
passing bouquets arranged
in their synthetic brightness
on my way to the open
floor plan of fresh breads,
sliced-to-order sandwich
meats, produce piled high
in raised beds for the reaching.
It felt like aisles and aisles
of freedom, freedom
from gluten, dairy, fat, all
the things an animal
can give, or the freedom
to have each one all at once
on a frozen pizza. It felt
like avoiding an old friend
at the checkout where
a plastic boundary keeps
my items mine, where the bag
I bring from home is
never enough to carry back
all I suddenly want.

Privilege

Into this sky which has
more airplanes
than other skies
I look and see half a dozen
small whitenesses passing
like tired stars
through the blue. I watch them
instead of watching
the woman swimming
in an oversized T-shirt that clings
to her body like slime, instead of
seeing the child splashing
in his inflatable sleeves
while his parents puff on
elaborate e-cigarettes.
Instead of speaking,
I lie back in my chair that's
turned to face the sun's full strength
and try to become browner.
In this sky, planes fly
low and heavy, back and
forth from the base,
practicing war. I'm afraid
I'm finally all right
knowing good things
in me have died.

Another Thing I'd Rather Not Know About Myself

is what a good soldier I'd make. A man
and woman come into the coffee shop
and talk about the dinner party menu
like it's the divorce settlement. I watch
them sit down, each ready to write
and argue, and he suggests jambalaya
and she says she's okay with that
to which he says *you don't sound okay*
with that and to answer she only asks
how it's spelled so she can type the decision
into her laptop, finally. And I don't mean
to say I'd be a good killer, just good
like she is at taking small deaths
in. He's shot. All right,
it's happened, I would think, because
that's what I've thought at every
bad turn in life: tire blown, it's
happened, money gone, it's happened,
pipes broken so the sewage has been
piling under the house for a month, it's
happened and we'll have to get
a pump in there to siphon it out.
Like the woman pecking now
without grudge at the keys that make
the word *jambalaya*, I'm quick to forgive
and get on. And I can see me there
on the battlefield, where nowadays
robots, I'm told, fall easily in
with the regiment and it's not so much
a field with two sides charging as a zone
in which every bit of live body heat

is fair game, where we're all
programmed for peace until a voice
echoes in our helmets that
we should *fire at will*. And fire we will,
all of us, and I think I'd be good
at staying willing, at letting each little
hit happen because there, it's happened
and isn't it little? Doesn't the grand
amount of flame-tinted shadow
on the infrared scanner make it so? Yes
I'd be such a good soldier. For
when the fire came back at us
and you fell next to me I'd forgive
the firer and get on with firing
at him. I'd forget about you
and engage. I'd be okay with that.

White Collar

Instead it's my job
to scrub the underside
of the dish sink. At

the end of a shift, tip-
laden, lonely, starched
white shirt spotted

with soup and grease,
like a mechanic I lie
on my back and scour

the metallic underbelly
where dinner morsels
and mold have amounted

to a layer of black glue,
lips pressed in a line
of defense against

whatever comes loose.
Later, in my kitchen
I soak the shirt in

my own sink, hang it
to dry, then iron
anew the one I wore

the shift before. Over
the radio, a voice says
the stocks have fallen

and fallen. Tomorrow
is the drip on the
tile floor I ignore.

Infomercial

You're not alone! a voice insists
when I can't find my keys
or the blanket slips from my ankles.
When I throw up my arms
and shake my head in surrender, he promises
I don't endure these sepia accidents
on my own. Everywhere, then,
there must be others who are fed up
with waking and mistaking
the glow of the streetlamps
for the headlights of someone
arriving. And in the quiet of no car doors
opening and closing, more
besides me wait in vain for the sounds
of being come back to. They
stand with me in the dark, watching
all that isn't moving out there
in the world, and they long with me
for a device to solve
all of it. By the light
of the television, the promise
of such cures feels as close as these
faux wood linoleum floors
underfoot. And when
I see the lives of my fellow sufferers
turn suddenly to color, I know
their remedy is also mine: I'm not
alone, so I reach for the phone.
I dial and imagine the voice
of the one who will answer, think
how he'll sound like
my very own forlorn inventor
sent to fix all my misplacements. I wait
for the click of the blessed receiver.
I hold for the sound
of the end of the difficult world.

Vivarium

So they'll feel at home

you stage for your pair of pet frogs
a daily storm, wake each morning

to pour darkness and fog

into their little world, broadcast
a soundtrack of thunder

paired with flashes of light

so they'll know it's time
to find one another

in the tempest, to mate.

We waited
so long for fall this year,

through too many weeks of

sales on bug spray and
stringy ears of corn, through

a September swelter that

stretched past the task
of spreading imitation cobwebs

over front yard shrubbery

so the neighborhood kids will know
we still honor the haunt.

Now winter is done

and what joy when you discover
a cache of eye-like eggs, find

a single black cell inside each

already beginning to cleave.
What consequence

when you hold them, god-like

in your palm
for the counting.

Tilt

Icons of illustrated cloud and sun
layer to say there will be some
of both, and some percent chance of
anything falling from the sky. By
these symbols I try to guess what's likely
today, whether we'll want to walk
a little in the spring dusk, or whether
another storm will come lunging
through the trees and streets ahead of
another cold front. You are
the brightest the days have been
in a long while. And while
the earth's oval journey, this boring
orbit around a star brings two
spheres closer, then farther apart,
something else a long time ago
decided this brimming, in-between
season: another planet smashing
into this one. Theia. Who knocked
us sideways. Some of her body
still bound up in our moon.

Threatless

After we pull into the drive
after we climb out of the car
after some silence between us
you reach
and rest your hand
on my neck at the base, your
thumb spread back beneath
my left ear,
other four fingers wrapped
and brushing the inside
of my collar, their
pressures as definite as a dune
whose grasses hold
the sandy hills together, keep
the beach a beach and
the ocean an ocean and
the world a world in which
you hold me
by the thing that holds up
my head, strange stem
we're not strong enough to use
at first, our heads
lolling and cradled in another's
hand, your mother's
hand, whose house
we're about to enter, whose
bay window
is big enough for her to see
us here in the shaded
spring eve, her son
holding a woman at the neck
in the threatless way he learned
from her, though of course
he doesn't remember

Clamor

Elsewhere air strikes carve
white gold through the night.
How they bloom and brandish
in the shadow of a warship
on the nightly news is meant
perhaps
to stir in my chest some vain-
glorious clamor, some cry.
Instead I remember you
washing the dishes while
a single tiny soap bubble
floated behind you, how you
didn't know it was there, and
perhaps
I craved the delicate secret
of the thing suspended
and temporary in the warm
kitchen glow, and wanted it to
stay mine, no matter the cost.

Code Red

While schoolchildren slip
like stolen hours into the corners
of the room, I turn
the half-disc of the lock
from horizon to high noon
then flip the little lever
of the light switch and like this
we have followed instructions,
we have done what we can.
The weather will be
what it is—several minutes
of sunshine or clouds,
maybe the kind of mist
you only know is falling
if you see it against gray road
or thick trees—inevitable,
exact result of every
wind, pressure, and breath
of earth's whole history
here rendered.
In darkness,
I remember the day
a heavy volume of landscapes
by Hitler came into the used
bookstore where my job
was to tenderly wipe down
the covers, then wrap the jackets
in clear plastic. Inside
were Austrian countrysides

and town squares, Alpine
villas and lakes as clear as
emptiness. A man
saw the world and sought ways
to make it look more like
how it feels to be lonely.
I remember this
now, now my job is to wait
for the noises to be
what they are, for the smells
and textures, the colors
of the air, of
the walls and floors.

Harvest

I am thinking terrible thoughts.
Dozens dead again and I am thinking
about what types of humans they were—
the gunman and the fallen. Yesterday
I was so happy to be greeting fall at last.
You wore a sweater with holes in it
and we had dinner with your aunt
who told us the story of how her son
had come to have half a heart. *I was
a bad mother*, she explained, *I never wanted
children*. The truth is he had heatstroke
and an undiagnosed defect. Little
murderous shadow, patient in the aorta
darkness. I am amazed, still, to be
beside you listening. That more and
more seasons gather and wane while
I'm allowed to remain near you and
near your sadnesses, familial tragedies.
Some days I wait for life to say *Enough*
and I practice the feeling of the world
narrowing again, of my body coursing
cold and my hands going limp, any
valuables I clutch returned with a
low rattle to the ground. Luck
will do that to you. Luck will stand on
its head and smile and you won't know
why and so you'll think of every other
explanation for what you deserve
or don't and you'll aim your weapon
accordingly. I am thinking about
who they were and who they were

trying to be. I am trying to turn luck
right-side up again. To make it look
me in the eye and say how these
blood-soaked rows came to be sown.
Otherwise how do I love you and
not love everyone at once? How do
I turn away while seed after seed
is buried and groomed? Luck making
his way, singing *Doom, doom, doom*.

Prix Fixe

Sunchoke
and fluke
for the first course, and
the impractical wine
pairing—we went for it.
What I mean is
we've been down in the dumps,
you and I, sick
of seeing wars start and
Star Wars ads
in the same breath, missile
Christmas gifts and mistletoe
gone brown
and brittle.
We figure we may
as well blow
half the rent on
Old World vintages
while we can.
Your favorite
is the honey-gold one
from Hungary,
which comes with
the chicken-liver tart
which I hate, but
if the two together
are the match we've
shelled out for
so be it.
What I mean is
it would've been nice

to have dinner with you
in a less ruthless season,
but as long as
I can wash this one
down with a nectar
nursed from a riverside vine
I'll be fine.
I'll sign
the check, tip
well, then drive home
smug as a man
in our valeted Toyota.

The World as It Is

Every disintegrating acre of me
deserves its yearly tending. Today, eyes
which haven't seen the world as it is
unassisted since childhood
have brought me here
to the optometrist where first
I watch a house drift in and out of focus
at the edge of a green distance, then
I endure that sudden puff of air they aim
at each pupil, then Dr. Barnes, who spoke
last year of a wife, daughter, skips
straight to asking which lenses make
the E's and M's and X's most vivid.
One, two. Two, three. Three, one.
It is February. The grocery
and drug stores have filled up
with reds and pinks and chocolates.
He is, I think, the sort of man
who'd never say if he was lonely.
Or I am the sort of woman who sees
the world as emptier than it is.
Two, three. Three, four. Four,
two. The choices are which is
better, or are they the same?

Omen

In a living room the size of
the President's heart
if his heart was one millionth of a star
instead of the dark-winged contents
of an ashtray we listen

to some urban bird caw,
to the upstairs neighbor's vacuum hum,
to a siren start and then give up,

and with fingertips warm
from holding a cup of the coffee
I brewed to begin our long, indoor day

you touch the skin at my hip
and a sick wind so soft
we didn't feel it begin begins

to make its way past our defenses
and I remember the day
I came home with

the dog, little black foundling
suddenly between us, and we knew
I had let in too much light. In

summer, some gold in
her brow, how she rubs
the raindrop of her nose into

turned soil, and the soft secret of
where in her barrel body
her heart really lives and beats—

every ultraviolet beam of her
scalds and then smolders beneath
a sky so thick with our exhales

one day long but not too long
from now we'll drown in
a flood of warm rivers set free
by her star, by its
very glare.

Nocturne

After I make my home dark
I wander through the few
quiet rooms and let
the bright blinking eyes
of the continuing electricity
take me in. The modem, forever
streaming its signals in and back
out again to the air of
the living room, flashes the language of
its six green indicators
into the dim, and I'm not
untouched. By the door,
the alarm pad keeps its emerald
beacon of earnest defense
burning on, and I'm not
vulnerable. And I remember
every thing is a thing
someone made, that
somewhere someone's job
is to place tiny bulbs inside
plastic bodies, that
someone else's is to decide
that firefly color, to sit
at a table shining under office light
and tell me which vividness
should tell me I am kept
safe, I am kept connected, even
as loneliness hums its generator
like a heart in a jar.

2.

Plasticity

Of course we might change
the brain, and the President might one
morning wake and learn the world
is huge and heartbroken.
Given practice, new neurons might meet
and send enough signals back and forth
and he'd see with his tongue,
map his bedroom
with taste. And wouldn't
that be something? The sour shape
of a bureau, of a quilt folded
at the foot of the bed
assembling like pointillism in
the night canvas of the blind man's
mind. That he might
find his way to the closet
and get dressed, still in darkness,
his ties singing out their colors
for him to choose from, that
he'd remember what blue is,
and that he'd be able after
some time to discover
the doorknob, to make his way
into the hall, the carpet still
rich under his feet
until onward into other rooms, homes
he might venture and see it all
anew. The volcanoes and
clouds, the highways, a man hidden
in plain sight amidst enemies.
He would have to dream, imagine it
all, over and over. It would
take a thousand years.

Seizure

I keep the light,
oceans, earth
safe inside my
pocket—inside
The Cloud, so
they can never be
lost. Then I am in
your arms, my body
wanting to wring
itself out, eyes
empty, saliva falling
like a necklace
from my mouth.
You say, It's okay
as my face turns
the color of the sea
in a storm, that
blue-gray wash
of asphyxia. In case
I can hear you
you say, It's okay—
everything is air

Beach Camping

Of the little bays of life lined up
at the edge of the world
our tent flaps along at the far end.
We spend the day
on the sand, calling the dog
back to us every several minutes
while a little ways up men work
to dredge and rebuild
what the last storm took
from the shoreline in time
for summer. Inside
bulldozer-like yellow vessels
they charge through gray waves,
drive hills of sea-earth
against the tide. Inside our lives
I spent days piling up
all we'd need here: cast iron,
French press, papers to burn.
The pile grew as we lived
and needed things—
no ideas but in them, after all.
My idea was
I wanted to be alone
with you, to watch you tear
and shove newspapers
beneath kindling, the light of it
on your face a poppy
orange, amber quiver. To help
this world suddenly pause as if
threatened by
some sickness, as if this

was our last warning: the moans
and spray of these machines
deepening their basin,
calling us back and back again
into the sea we crawled
out of, our lungs
only gill-clouds, half-formed,
gasping.

The Drowning

I miss you. I wandered away above
the sea caves, walked along the grassy
cliff for so long the tide came in, and now
it laps over the cuffs of my jeans, now
to get back I'm wading into the
deepening black and feeling a rock's curve
press into the arch of my footstep. It
feels like your heel pressing there
as it did so many mornings as we woke
each other slowly, with such small pressures
the noises of the day beginning outside
seemed to soften. Where are you?
Were you there that groggy afternoon
I crawled inside a playhouse in my
childhood city? You'd remember the
pink light, how the plastic walls
seemed to breathe back their chemicals
into the warm air. The bricks underfoot
were damp; the dirt between them had let
a low moss come up, softening each step.
An earthworm squirmed next to my
blue sneaker. Were you watching as I lifted
a doll's cup and pressed its lip down
into the worm's soft body, splitting him
in two? I was thinking about skunks,
how they spray their invisible stink
when they sense danger, and octopuses
spilling their clouds of ink into the sea,
and about bees stabbing their poisonous
rear ends into flesh and then dying
anyway. I watched both ends of the worm

writhe as if with renewed life and
believed one had become two bodies.
Now I see an anemone's eye close,
and now the water wraps and pulls at
my waist. Are you waiting on the northern
shore, where I began? When I went back
to the playhouse days later, only one
worm was waiting. Headless, I finally
understood, for it was shriveled and dead
in the foyer of my imaginary life. If
the other survived, crawled away
alone, I never understood how. How,
as the sandy floor falls out from
under me, does a body float to shore?

Love Sick

Only one thing remained reachable, close and secure
amid all losses: language [...] it went through. It gave me no
words for what was happening, but went through it all. Went
through and could resurface, 'enriched' by it all.

—Paul Celan

1.

What happens is you long for an end

to loneliness and for so long the longing

becomes as powerful and brown as the city river

Jeff Buckley drowned in or the one John Berryman

jumped into, either way the Mississippi, only

Buckley waded in from the bank of a branch

outside Memphis while Berryman leapt from

a bridge in Minneapolis in January, either way

what started as longing becomes an impulse

to immerse, the same one you feel each time

the river slows around a bend where a body

stands promising to keep the same secrets

as your body, and you want to swim in that

water, yes, even when the water is the war of

a country whose name is a body, or when it's

the stolen fortunes of a past whose crown

is a body, and either way the water is warm,

inflammation even in winter, even to Berryman

as his Mr. Bones voice went silent at last, and

warm as well for Buckley who walked calm

into the current, floated off singing the chorus

of Led Zeppelin's "Whole Lotta Love" while

a body listened from the shore as the song got

quieter, quieter

2.

which is how all this began, this climb

toward no summit, this life of poetry which

once prompted a friend to ask why do so

many poets off themselves, like what's this

disease that makes you see an oven as so much

more than an oven, and why do you set yourselves

afloat and then claim surprise when the river's

waters are stronger than yours? The friend didn't

say it that way, though—you're saying it better

now, and either way one thing that really is true

is you were floating a river right that very

moment, adrift down a dirty Chattahoochee

and so maybe this metaphor began right then

and there, and right now and here you have both

vehicle and tenor, lucky you, you've solved a

mystery akin to the question of who programs

the street lights, tells them to turn off one

minute later each morning as we sink

toward winter

3.

which is something you wondered about once

while walking the dog within one of those instants

you recklessly make into meaning, which is why

you take to journeying and see for instance

a movie in France, Civil War melodrama which

in Toulouse helps you see the absurdity of the

concept of a country, or why you look through

the black lines of the Spirit Warrior sculpture at

Little Bighorn, at the blue Montana sky behind

and decide the bronze horsemen look like

tributaries trying to hold in an ocean, or why

you stand at the overlook at Crater Lake, read

a placard about the volcano's eruption and the

eight thousand years of rain that followed and

figure out time is only endless consequence; or

why you make love, why afterward you try to

describe the lingering scent as cinnamon and

salt water—it's all so you can churn for a while

in each whirlpool until a new current comes,

one that's quick and deep, flicker invisible

and eager, as if airborne

4.

and that fever, that morning-lavender

twilight-opposite bright, beguiling begonia,

it carries you for miles, miles of appetite-less

delirium. You think you know the weight of

a body beside your body ready to reach down

and pull you up by the shoulder of your life vest

if ever a wave tries to swallow you whole, you

think you know the change in air around a body

as it bends to touch damp hands to the bank's

earthsoil, to bring its metal-silt taste to your tongue

and you think you know the weaponry of a

body's eyes in the dark of a quiet room, how

something sea missile-like launches and

lands in your bloodstream and you think

speaking each certainty will keep the wound

from worsening, will rinse this opening in

warm water, pack it with gauze and ready its

bandage to be kissed, be measured

5.

but you've forgotten, meanwhile, the night-day

highway of that tornado in South Dakota, its

green flag warning like spilled watercolor, you've

forgotten the river is *belonging* without the *be*, that

it is the trying to be, the endless calculated attempt

to keep the body nearby, to never let the body

know yours is a body, too, and that the language

you share is the language of Masters, men who

also only wanted to keep other bodies nearby

and loyal, who named flora species after each

other and so you say you hate loyalty, can't trust

its unconditionality and its song, and you swear

not to sing it but some songs aren't music, some

songs are funnels of wind and ruptured atmosphere

and the surface they curl toward and suck from is

the river, always the same river, and the lyrics

are *keep*, *stay*, *hold on*—words you don't sing

but drink

6.

and that black milk you drink it even though

it's mud-sweet, the way a birdbath's pool

might taste or better yet the beads of sugar water

in the silver dollar-sized hummingbird feeder

you hold in the palm of your hand hour after

hour toward a body that hovers above the river,

wings imperceptible, always about to leave.

You think you know at least how to hold this

one here, that ceremony will be enough, thing

created to be counted on what with its series of

steps, one word meaning another word meaning

another as if immune to erosion, yes, you've

mistaken the drug for the cure and forgotten

even the clearest snowmelt contains soil from

the mountainside and that at night when there's

nothing but frail moonlight to see by you are

holding something obsidian: black milk left

behind—you drink it

7.

as if to get well you could swallow your own

suffering, follow it down into the nightspace

of your gut so as to understand and withstand

its late recipe, to finally hold the warm loaf

of it in your hands (this poem), and there

you go into the kitchen again where it feels

most possible, this serving up of yourself, this

offering you hope might help you become like

the ghosts whose sad ends, so often sicknesses,

nailed them to the world like words, yes, you

only wanted to be as eventual, definite—like

one of those dead-end streets you loved as

a child—place where pavement ends and the

body stands pathless as if the woods beyond

aren't also a route, and a disappearing one, as

if blending into a black tree line he'd ask you

to follow

8.

which finds you back at the riverbank, edge

of the next-best traceable route to the sea

where the longing becomes the missing and

the missing is rain like Washington's rain

downy as fleece and subtle. Yes, in another

specific America you're alive and snug in a

valley of old growth fir trees where low clouds

churn and give milk, blue milk this time,

because the sky is a metaphor, too—

wide sea turned back on itself which is how

one word can mean nothing and another

too much, how you and the body each meant

something else when you said the word *love*,

how now the one remedy left is to ask this

big ceiling to load its rooms on a lever

effort-heavy with farms, highways and city

parks, airfields, libraries, delis and capitol

steps, ski lifts and schools so your love for

the world will send you back skyward,

diving-board high and soon swimming back

in home's evening, late summer, streetlights

still off, trying to name the together-sound

of cicadas and interstate, only now knowing

it's only me left listening

9.

so forgive me: I know by now you are lost

as I have been lost in the telling of all this, this

saturation, disintegration of so many soul-cells,

in the naming of what has happened, of what

will happen again. You wanted to keep your

head above water and drown at the same

time. You, Speaker, wanted to swim alongside

me, Body, and in doing so swim with the

deadness of language, so you drove off in

the vehicle of a metaphor and smashed into

a tree, or soared over the rail of a bridge, and

you have been waiting for me, Body, to break

the window and swim us to the surface

10.

so forget Celan, the Seine. Remember instead

the bedspread's sea, calm now you are alone

again. Rest. There were always women who

loved these men and those they loved after.

Rest. The world has always been named with

translator's betrayals, this distance between

the current and the shore. Long-hauler, rest

with gratitude for the antibodies that dance

within you now, rest-less. The world learns.

We have staked our lives on this. As by now

we've learned more about what Buckley sang

as he walked calm into the current, floated off

while a body listened from the shore as the

song got quieter, quieter—his too was mostly

stolen from Muddy Waters, and Willie Dixon

before him, and watered down with each thief,

molecules mutated so they'd fit intricately into

his cells, which is what you've been trying to

say all along, you just couldn't find the words.

3.

The Listenings

I didn't know it was supposed to be
this bad, I said of the ice storm.
I was thinking of how night
surrounds a house on the coast, of
how the ferocious-sounding sea
carries on crashing while humans look out
and see nothing, how all we perceive are
the sounds of the world changing
wave by wave without us.
That night the world changed
raindrop by raindrop
and sounded like any rain except
for a faint and steady hiss
as the glass hardened over our cars,
our power lines, our oak trees.
As the roads became
impassable, slick rivers.
I didn't know we were supposed to
become so entirely stranded.
Thus the feeling as I woke
and saw a new kind of light
out the window, a white-heavy shine
over everything. That sense that
we'd lived through something mighty
without being afraid or even
aware. All night with you next to me,
the world was becoming
a diamond. And somewhere else
an inlet formed, and all the listenings
in the end were poor guesses, weak
theories of what that thunderous a tide
could've carried away.

Diagnosis

Yesterday a little camera
slipped inside me and let me
look around. Turns out
a body is all walls and debris—
a morning sky behind tiny petals
floating over the windshield
like snow. But it is newly
spring, when bright winds spin
delicate white dots down from
the trees, around the roads.
Nothing will freeze for
a while. Inside, everything
was empty. Outside the sky
was thick as flesh, the bruised
white of an interim dawn.
And there was still time.

Dark

Schools gone dark. On the last day
we told the children to take everything
home, supervised as they emptied dark
lockers of books, loose pages, mirrors.
I don't drive past the dark windows and
halls, missing it. I make dark the living
room and fill it back up with the light of
a movie. Something about creatures who
stalk in the dark, thrive on its blankness.
But I go to bed before the end, when
dark returns to the screen with its list
of names. I sleep in dark, but shove
voices in my ears that belong to bodies
who sat in lit rooms a good while ago
to discuss science, loss. Even sunrises—
I sleep through them now, can't stand
that semi-dark slide into the worsened
day. Dark soil in the garden beds, in
the houseplants, spilled on the kitchen
floor. The dark fur of the dog so soft
I'd skin her to make myself a coat if I
didn't love the rest of her so desperately.
Dark thoughts like that in my head
all day. Dark mode so the screens are
gentler on the eyes. Not that they feel
any strain—no dark itch in the pupil.
If anything I feel so much the same—
no new humid night sets its dark down
in my swallow (the sickness), nor does
any heart-wound turn rotten and raw.
I am the dark's pale rider, indifferent

and slow. By the time schools reopen,
dark won't be anything on which to
remark. A girl will open her locker and
out dark will pour and she'll think how
she's learned it. Dark homework. Dark
that has spent all these days staring
into a left-behind mirror at itself, stirred
to cloud at last, to a downpour about
to make the day cool and blue, make all
this a yesterday. Her shadowy backpack.

I Still Go to the Movies

But to be alone in the dark
and light of a life

not my own, I forget
isn't always a peace.

Sometimes the same seams
come apart in real life

and I have to admit
happiness is the warmth

of a kitchen or the slant
sun of winter—

a medicine
here to offer its dose

and then vanish. Still
as with the dog

whose waste I carry daily
to the garbage

I have to pretend.
That I won't help her die

one day, either
by failure or mercy, and

soon. That the well in me
won't run dry and require

the flicker of a theater
to fill it back up.

Livestream

Sometimes snow
drifts and lands in watery blurs
on the glass at the front of the train
and a thin black blade passes
in swift intervals over the windshield
makes the view clear and sharp
for a partial-second
makes a fir tree's limbs
specific as we pass
over the next tract
of Norway
but most days
the scene is unobscured
the banks along our path solid white
but for the broad
stone shoulders undusted
and at the sight of their shadows
violet cloaks abandoned
along the bank
a passenger types
I have known how to live
in loneliness many years ago
and the rest of us
recognize
and nod

Living History

When I think about time
I think about Colonial Williamsburg, how
you can go back to the 1770s and
smell the horses and listen to the wagons rolling
off of red brick onto dirt road
and still feel exactly alone in America
before America even existed.
You can go to the craft demonstration
and make eyes at the man
who melts pig fat into candle wax, fall for him
even though he would've died
by now, in one of the wars
that was coming.
You can dream him
into any hour, any decade,
despite the slow and terrible rotation,
the turning away of everything
from what you first thought it was.
That's why when I think about longing
I think of the people I've known the longest,
of how we've traveled so far
from the days when we, too, were only
colonists, eager to settle
the tillable plains, to tame the wilds
of before love was a country. Which is why
all my best loves are immediate strangers:
we meet young, or old in a place
that looks and smells like youth did
and what we each love most is knowing nothing
of who the other one will be.
And inside our New World

we feel time lie down and swell
into an era that'll be rebuilt, maybe
centuries later. We're sure someone
will put on these old-fashioned clothes and
reenact our artisan lust, and
a whole lonely people will come
to visit the town where
our ravage began.

Living Alone

I'll be a Woman With a Drill, not
a Woman With a Neighbor With a Drill.
Because things will always need tightening
and who has the hand strength
to turn the screws themselves? Of course
I'll also be a Woman With an Iron, but
this won't make me any less free
from the Man Next Door. When he
sees me in my pressed blouse when we pass
in the hallway, he'll swoon and I'll
barely look up. I'll take baths
with the window open, and I'll listen
as the people outside leave and arrive
and the only sign I'm there will be the steam
that rises upward through the screen.
Even when it's quieter at evenings,
after I check the mail and no one
but the bank has remembered me
I won't complain. The meatloaf
I'll make will last my lone appetite
a week, and I'll put off cleaning the pan.
And to keep the relapse at bay, before bed
I'll swallow just the right dose
of desire: I'll think of you, because
I can think of you if I want.
I know what's best for me, how much
haunt my heart can endure.
As I'll manage in spite of the one blade
of the ceiling fan that's tilted

off its hinges, I'll manage
with the thought of you hanging
gracelessly on. I won't take the drill
and dismantle the skeleton—I'll get by
with it holding on there, useless and
off-center, like some petal about to break off
in the breeze of the air conditioner.

Lesson

Here a honeysuckle air
bathes a piece of the path
I take to work, stretch of pavement soaked
in the sweet butter scent of sunlight
and earth spinning their chemistry
inside each little flower to
lure in the bees. I pass through it
on my way to teach adolescents
history and grammar, the mistakes
of great men and punctuation, how
the placement of a pen stroke
might disrupt altogether the intent
of a sentence, an imperative
object. I put worry in their hearts,
then try to calm them with promises
of things not getting any easier.
Meanwhile another creature
will only have to land
on the delicate end of a single
open calyx to cancel the debts of
distance, separation. All
of what the great men couldn't
manage. All the purposes of a comma
lost, unneeded, lovely gone.

This Century

> *Maybe, if I had a choice,*
> *I would remember no one,*
> *But walk on the frail water*
> *Over the floating floors of*
> *A madhouse*
> *—Larry Levis*

Maybe this madhouse
is the one I've been swimming
toward all month—month of
the anniversaries of Stonewall and
Judy Garland both saying no
more, no more of this
please, June. So
I spend an hour poring
over this poem, its strange
movements from story to sad
memory, its soft announcements
of great truths, its visit to Ireland
and then its ending of sky.
If I had a choice,
I would sit down with
Larry and ask him what one
thing was daggered into him that
day he wrote it, and did he
get it out? But he was gone
before I even owned
this book, even
before I first read it

which was with a different copy,
library copy hard-backed and
jacketless with a single
snowflake imprint
on its front
though the title said
Stars not *Snow*, but Larry, you
could pull tricks like that, like say
stars and snow are the same
and everyone believed you
which must have felt
very strange.
To build a madhouse
for yourself out of moths
and train smoke and then all these
strangers show up saying
Thanks for the invite!
And it's true their
faces are not
any you remember
but they seem to know yours
which is an ache that's even sharper
than wanting to forget the ones
you worry you didn't cherish
enough, though of course
you did, Larry.
You stood
in a barroom with
beautiful lunatics and sang
your own "Over the Rainbow" and
I only wish I'd been there.
This century sucks.
Everyone is
a memory.

The Night of the Ghost

Gardenia hasn't hung this heavy
in years. And I bet the lightning bugs
will be back sooner than usual.
Ever since the city shut down
the noise above their ground nests
has so diminished they'll think they're
waking up within countryside calm.
Last summer I holed up in a house
in the dense woods upstate and
watched a square ghost fold in on
itself—geometric specter on
the rough face of a big oak. I was
there to make poems, but I
made myself crazy instead, chasing
and trapping big insects all day
only to return them to the outside
world they'd snuck free from—wasps
and beetles who crept in through
cracks in the doors and window frames,
anywhere warped wood pulled away
from where it once lined up flush.
The night of the ghost, I didn't sleep
because a dozen fireflies crawled in, one
by one through an opening around
the window AC. So maybe I was
seeing things, some glow of a world
I didn't belong to, like them: In the pitch
dark, the temperature panel burned
lime-bright, a false beckoning.
Then the ghost made itself smaller
and smaller against the tree until
it was gone. All those days, all
the days and nights since, and all
I've written down to describe it are
these two swift sentences:
The animals take their turn.
The wind has never smelled this sweet.

Nocturne

After I make my home dark
this time down to every bead and
thread of red and green
on the clock face, the thermostat,
this midsummer night
settles, assumes
its own tepid burden in
its branches which shimmer, yes
which send down dozens of tremulous
glimmers from the fireflies
high in the trees and
soft upon the window screen
saying with light-words
We are surging with tenderness
and plight, we who wait
for our season
and who survive such
long underground days on
our way to be mated and most
of all, named. By scientists
who fashioned from
Latin and categories
my favorite—Lampyridae.
Lamp, here am I.
Here am I.

Poem

At last I laid my hands
on the one about

the airport and the lover.
And I know I'm not supposed

to let a poem tell me
my life, but let me explain.

It is pre-dawn dark, the moon
is still in the sky

and is my favorite kind
of crescent and I'm sipping

something hot and
eating cold wedges of fruit

and remembering the first time
I held this book, walked

home from the library
reading

which isn't something
I normally do but

that afternoon the sidewalks
were just empty enough

and I hardly
had to cross any streets

and the poem was
murky. Wide, opaque

puddle of things I'd never
quite felt. And now

that it is too late for stars and
too soon for sun

the only things up there besides
the moon are

satellites and planes
carrying signals and lovers

and one of them
mine. Poem,

poem whose waters have rushed
over the rocks in me

all these years, could you
run clear now?

No, it turns out.
But you are as necessary

an unquenched mystery
as ever.

ACKNOWLEDGMENTS

Thank you to the following publications where these poems originally appeared:

Alaska Quarterly Review: "Diagnosis"
The American Poetry Review: "Another Thing I'd Rather Not Know About Myself,"
   "Living History," "Harvest"
Bookstore Clerks & Significant Others, Tsunami Press: "Poem"
Bennington Review: "Code Red"
The Cincinnati Review: "Tilt"
Colorado Review: "Livestream"
The Georgia Review: "Lesson"
The Glacier: "The Night of the Ghost," "This Century"
The Laurel Review: "Infomercial," "The World as It Is," "I Still Go to the Movies"
The New Yorker: "Clamor," "Privilege," "Dark"
Off the Coast: "Living Alone"
The Paris Review: "Nocturne" [After I make my home dark / I wander
   through the few]"
Radar Poetry: "The Listenings"
Scoundrel Time: "Plasticity"
THRUSH Poetry Journal: "White Collar"
Yemassee Journal: "The Drowning," "Seizure"

Thank you as well to my schools, my teachers, and to my parents, Jay and Julie.

Photo: Matthew Spaulding

Elly Bookman grew up in downtown Atlanta and earned an MFA from the University of North Carolina at Greensboro. Since 2013 she has worked as an educator while consistently publishing her poetry in some of the most widely-read markets in the country, including *The New Yorker*, *The Paris Review*, and *The American Poetry Review*. She was the recipient of the first annual Stanley Kunitz Memorial Prize from *The American Poetry Review* and the Loraine Williams Poetry Prize from *The Georgia Review*. She teaches middle and high school at The Paideia School in Atlanta.